Tactical Motherhood

Claiming Victory on the Home Front

ROBIN LUDWIG

ISBN: 9798833131688

More from the author:
www.robinludwigwrites.com
www.waitingpassionately.blog

Holy Bible translations:
Complete Jewish Bible, David H. Stern,
Messianic Jewish Publishers, 1998.
New International Version, Zondervan, 2011.
New Living Translation, Tyndale House Publishers, 2000.

Reverential capitalization reflects the author's stylistic choice.

for my Abba,

who pulled me from the miry clay

and called me beloved

Table of Contents

Acknowledgements

Rev. Dr. James Ward Hudson, DMin, LPC, MEd, MDiv & The Amazing Vivian Hudson, for lives devoted to ceaseless prayer, spiritual warfare, unconditional love, theological input, editing, and blazing a worthy trail for me to follow. Mark, Asher, & Keane Ludwig, for carrying me through with your prayers during drill weekends and deployments; and for unconditional love and grace in the midst of writing. Kailee Tidball, for fervent prayer, constant encouragement, and being the Anne to my Diana. Laura Jeffreys, for godly wisdom, life-giving friendship, and always being willing to listen. Elizabeth Huffman, for being a grammatical ninja, phenomenal tutor, and a godly example of biblical strength under fire. Classical Conversations Colleyville Community, for being the best tribe any mama could ever have, for loving my family through deployments, and for the honor of doing life with you. Heather Fuller, for brilliant ideas and writing expert cover copy; your incandescent happiness will change the world. Duncan Ray Brannan, for showing up to divine appointments, encouraging words, and eagle-eyed editing. Rebecca Friedlander & The Potter's House Creative Ministries, for launching this vision. Sally Clarkson, for looking me directly in the eyes and telling me I'm capable, and for allowing me the great honor of pouring your tea…after years of you pouring into my life.

INTRODUCTION

My life is a tapestry woven of floral fabrics and camouflage, accessorized with dangly earrings and combat boots. I have an odd assortment of dainty China cups for afternoon tea, as well as industrial-strength coffee mugs sturdy enough to withstand the apocalypse. Without any hesitation—and with great enthusiasm—I can wax poetic over Winston Churchill and Jane Austen. I'm equal parts wife, homeschool mom, teacher, and Air Force First Sergeant. My experiences allow me to see the world through a lens that has been fashioned from intense training. My passion for Jesus keeps me steeped in scripture and prayer. I have one foot firmly planted in a combat boot, and the other deeply rooted in Christ. That unique combination has shaped me in ways I will never fully comprehend, but I stand firm in the belief that God knew exactly what he was doing when he knit me together.

God has called me to rally the troops for battle. I'm not referring to members of the armed forces, I'm passionately beseeching mothers to answer this call. Whether we realize it or not, we were commissioned for service the day we entered motherhood. Through scripture, well-known military maxims, and personal stories, I will lead the charge through *Tactical Motherhood* to prepare you for the battle at hand. While writing these pages, God placed Habakkuk 2:2 on my heart.

Then ADONAI answered me; he said, "Write down the vision clearly on tablets, so that even a runner can read it." Habakkuk 2:2 (CJB)

Since returning home from recent deployments, I've felt such an urgency to equip mothers for spiritual battle in their homes. This book is intentionally brief. My goal is not to add to the overwhelm, but to be your wingman as you partner with Christ in the midst of motherhood. Anyone who has encountered a military field manual will have noticed they tend to be easily portable and ready for action. This purposefully concise field guide helps you make an immediate kingdom-impact on your family.

Each chapter begins with one of my military life-lessons, and how it impacts motherhood. Then we delve into scripture to see God's message for mothers. After spending time in prayer, you will partner with Jesus in a time of reflection. There is space provided "To Remember" what God is speaking to you, as well as plenty of room to write your reflections.

In a week's time—including Sabbath margin—you'll have fashioned an actionable, impactful, and personalized battle plan for your family. If one week sounds overwhelming in this season of life, then take each chapter one week at a time. On days when motherhood feels like an uphill battle, when reinforcements are nowhere in sight, you can refer back to tactical plans you handcrafted with Jesus. When your heart is heavy and the enemy is trying to distract you from your mission of motherhood, review these pages to remind yourself that you are not alone.

The enemy is out for blood, my friends. He is unashamedly after our children. He brought the battle to our doorstep, but we will defend our homes and families through the power of the Holy Spirit. *Tactical Motherhood* calls us to stand in the gap. To take up the sword. To lay waste to culture's claims on our children. Under the guidance of the Commander of Heaven's Armies, we will not falter or fail. We will claim victory on the home front!

1. Raise your Right Hand

So do not fear, for I am with you; do not be dismayed, for I am your God. I will strengthen you and help you; I will uphold you with my righteous right hand.
Isaiah 41:10 (NIV)

I have nothing to offer but blood, toil, tears, and sweat.
Winston Churchill

My initiation into the military involved much screaming, sweating, and sleepless nights. The same can be said of my entrance into motherhood. Remembering my first day of Basic Military Training now brings a smile to my face—mostly because I know I'll never have to do that again—but there were no smiles to be had on that day in March of 2003. I was heartily greeted by angry instructors, yelling so loudly their veins were bulging out of their necks. They ushered my group of young women up to the dorm rooms, where a high-spirited female sergeant loudly commanded us to get completely undressed and high-tail it directly to the showers. The other girls and I side-eyed one another for a panicked nano-second, just long enough to silently regret our life choices and ask ourselves, "Is this really happening?"

It was.

And we did.

I can tell you from firsthand experience that nothing builds camaraderie quite like shared fear and being thrown into a cold shower before you get around to *How do you do?* or *Where are you from?* Our civilian clothes were swiftly locked away; we were given uniforms, combat boots, and new names. I was no longer Robin, but Trainee. In one fell swoop, life as I knew it was over.

Perhaps you felt that way during your first foray into motherhood. No amount of reading, planning, or advice could ever fully prepare you for all that motherhood would throw your way. The sleepless nights, changing hormones, diapers, cluster feedings, teething discomfort, croupy coughs, and on and on and on…it's not for the faint of heart. Life as you knew it changed in the blink of an eye.

The same can be said of Queen Esther. This young orphaned Jewish girl was being raised by her devout Jewish uncle. This pair of unlikely heroes found themselves far from home in the midst of exile. Her given name, Hadassah, is Hebrew for myrtle. The myrtle represents God's divine establishment of the Jewish people, and is a symbol of His enduring promises.

Where once there were thorns, cypress trees will grow.
Where nettles grew, myrtles will sprout up. These events will
bring great honor to the LORD*'s name; they will be an*
everlasting sign of his power and love.
Isaiah 55:13 (NLT)

The book of Esther tells us Hadassah was *taken* from her Uncle Mordecai's home and placed in pagan King Xerxes' harem.

As a result of the king's decree, Esther, along with many other young women, was brought to the king's harem at the fortress of Susa... Esther 2:8 (NLT)

She went from a Torah-focused, kosher lifestyle under Mordecai's protection to a lascivious fortress ruled by an impetuous king. Her Persian name, Esther, means star and hidden. Hadassah left all she knew to be hidden away for a time. She was given a new name, new clothes, and—for a while—had to hide her Jewish identity. Through it all, God was with her. We, too, live in exile as we journey through life as mothers. Hebrews 13:14 reminds us this world is not our home.

For this world is not our permanent home; we are looking forward to a home yet to come. Hebrews 13:14 (NLT)

You have been called and commissioned into the ranks of motherhood! You've been given a new name. (Mom! Mommy! Mama! Mum! Moooommmma!) You have answered the high and holy calling to steward souls in the midst of a fallen world. Our culture may not look like Persia during the time of exile, but it is a harsh and weary place. The very word "mother" is being legislated to "birthing person" while men are being emasculated left and right. Children are not viewed as God-given blessings, but nuisances who aren't given the basic right to life. The enemy has launched an all-out assault on families. We cannot wait for someone to stand in the gap for us. Lace up your boots, Warrior Mama, it's time to fight for your family!

This fight begins inside the very walls of your home. The enemy works to infiltrate when your guard is down. His plan of attack is to lull you and your family into quiet resignation, letting culture dictate your priorities. This thief wants to rob us of our time, sanity, and compassion. He wants us to run ourselves ragged while we attempt to keep up with sports practices, community events, playdates, laundry, dishes, cooking, and cleaning. If our lives are at a constant level of overwhelm, we leave ourselves open to attack. If we're too focused on putting our children in every possible enrichment activity, we leave them vulnerable to the enemy's schemes. It's *your* home and *your* motherhood that makes all the difference. Partnering with Jesus to release His peace, purpose, and protection over your family will impact your great-great-great grandchildren.

Prayer

God, help me to view motherhood as an integral part of Your divine design. Strengthen me for the battle at hand. I ask the Holy Spirit to reveal Himself in every aspect of my parenting. I stand firm in Your word, and find my identity only in You. Thank You for clothing me in Your strength and dignity. In Jesus' name, I declare that I am a warrior who is equipped for training my children in righteousness. In Jesus' gracious name, amen.

Call to Arms: Motherhood Creed

Each branch of the service has their own creed that defines the core characteristics of who they are and what they value. Throughout the centuries, Christians have relied on The Nicene Creed and The Apostle's Creed to remind them of their firm foundation in Christ. It's time to create your own Motherhood Creed! Ask God to speak to your heart, to refute every lie you've ever believed, and to reveal His truth. (For reference purposes, I have included my own Motherhood Creed on page 12. Rest assured, yours does not need to look anything like mine.)

1. Research and write down the meaning of your name. You may choose your first, middle, last, or a combination of all three names!

____

____

____

____

____

____

____

____

____

____

____

____

____

____

____

2. Write down a Bible verse(s) that you've held near and dear. What scripture has God brought to mind over and over? In the darkest of times, what scripture has anchored you to the Father?

3. Make a list of strengths and spiritual gifts God has given you. If you feel unsure where to begin, recall life-giving words spoken to you by fellow Christ followers. Read through 1 Corinthians 12 and ask the Holy Spirit to reveal your unique gifting.

4. Use the meaning of your name(s), key words from your chosen scripture, and your gifts to write a brief Motherhood Creed. Consider your values, mission, and goals for your family.

Robin's Motherhood Creed

1. My first, middle, and last names mean victorious, courageous, and noble warrior.

2. One of my life scriptures is Isaiah 35:3-4.

With this news, strengthen those who have tired hands, and encourage those who have weak knees. Say to those with fearful hearts, "Be strong, and do not fear, for your God is coming to destroy your enemies. He is coming to save you."

3. Some of my gifts and strengths include faith, encouragement, intercession, and teaching.

4. I am a courageous noble warrior who is victorious in spirit! God has gifted me with supernatural faith and life-giving words of encouragement in order to bring freedom to my family. Through joyful intercession and passionate teaching, I will strengthen those with tired hands and weak knees. I will partner with the Holy Spirit to say to those with fearful hearts, "Be strong, and do not fear, for your God is coming to destroy your enemies. He is coming to save you!"

2. Understand your Authority

I will give you the keys of the kingdom of heaven; whatever you bind on earth will be bound in heaven, and whatever you loose on earth will be loosed in heaven.
Matthew 16:19 (NIV)

My mother was the most beautiful woman I ever saw. All I am I owe to my mother. I attribute my success in life to the moral, intellectual and physical education I received from her.
George Washington

With each passing year of military service, I gain more responsibility and achieve higher rank. During those early years, I was subject to many authority figures. As the rank on my sleeves and wrinkles on my forehead increased, I transitioned into one of those authority figures. I remember one instance in Basic Training where I waltzed into a Chief Master Sergeant's office and promptly asked a dumb question. In doing so, I had played leap frog over several leaders in my chain of command, and earned myself a magnificent verbal assault. My ears rang for a good hour after that life lesson. Fast forward twenty years, now *my* office is where the younger enlisted members show up to ask questions.

Back then, I had not yet earned the right to walk into an authority figure's office without first going through several other checks and balances. I needed permission. Twenty years later, my rank and position provide me access to top leadership, without needing to ask permission.

As a daughter of Christ, *you* have unmitigated access to God. Without an ounce of hesitation, guilt, or fear, you can approach the throne of grace with confidence.

Let us then approach God's throne of grace with confidence, so that we may receive mercy and find grace to help us in our time of need. Hebrews 4:16 (NIV)

The authority you have was purchased by the blood of Jesus – it is worth everything! With that in mind, I implore you to understand the massive responsibility that comes with the title of Mother: **Do not abdicate your authority.** No one else has the ability or authority to speak into your child's life the way you do. This is a God-given authority that must *never* be abandoned. What we, as mothers, do with that authority has eternal value. Unequivocally, I am speaking of our roles as grace-givers, truth-speakers, and hope-brokers. We should be fountains of life-giving encouragement that lead our children to the feet of Jesus. Our words have the ability to build up or tear down.

The tongue has power over life and death; those who indulge it must eat its fruit. Proverbs 18:21 (CJB)

What "fruit" are we feeding our children?

What words do they hear coming out of our mouths on a regular basis?

It's you, Dear Mama. Not the government. Not the coach. Not the teacher. Not the preacher. Not the cool youth minister or high-energy camp counselor. You wield this awesome level of authority. This authority belongs to you, and must be properly exercised under the banner of Christ. It is with brokenhearted lament that I look at the world around me and see countless mothers who have abdicated their precious authority. This is happening in the Church. We can see countless examples of mothers giving up, throwing in the towel, and letting others have the primary role of speaking into her child's life.

When we fail to speak life-giving biblical words of wisdom; when we fail to pray without ceasing; when we do not interject God's truth into culture's lies, we open the door to the enemy.

None of us would willingly open the door to a thief on our threshold. Yet that's exactly what happens when we abdicate our maternal authority. Satan is waiting to fill that void in our children's hearts with words that steal, kill, and destroy (John 10:10). Culture is waiting to fill the gaps in their minds with toxic lies. Warrior Mama, it's your words of biblical affirmation and love that have the utmost potential to save lives. If you struggle with speaking life over your children, invite the Holy Spirit into this area. Make Psalm 19:14 your heart's cry.

May the words of my mouth and the mediation of my heart be pleasing to you, O LORD, my rock and my redeemer.
Psalm 19:14 (NLT)

As mothers, we must be about Kingdom business at all times in the lives of our children. We are imperfect human beings who will fall short, there's no getting around that fact. However, it's in those times of failure that we cling to God's word and continue to speak life over our family. When my boys were two and four years old, I began speaking biblical affirmations over them each morning. Those seeds I diligently sowed in their hearts years ago have taken root, sprouted, and are now bearing fruit.

My words alone did not have any special power, but the scripture I spoke over them had the power of Heaven behind it. It was mustard seed faith in action. I bathed their hearts and minds in God's life-giving words. My husband and I have bookended our sons' days with biblical affirmations and blessings for as long as I can remember. Before they drift off to sleep each night, I kiss them and whisper the Aaronic Blessing into their ears.

The LORD bless you and keep you; the LORD make his face shine on you and be gracious to you; the LORD turn his face toward you and give you peace.
Numbers 6:24-26 (NIV)

On days I mess up and lose my temper, my children aren't left with empty words or echoes of frustration. By the time I inevitably mess up (usually by noon), they have already heard ten loving statements of biblical affirmation. Every night as I tuck them in bed, they fully expect to receive their blessings—no matter what kind of day we've all had. They rely on the authority of my loving words to affirm, restore, and fill their hearts with love.

Prayer

God, I commit my mind, heart, and mouth to You. In the same way You purified Isaiah's lips with a hot coal, I ask the Holy Spirit to do the same for me. May I fluently speak life over my children. Guide me in my role as a mother. Teach me how to steward well the authority You've given me. I repent where I've abdicated that authority in the past. Bring about supernatural restoration and healing in my family's relationships. In Jesus' powerful name, amen.

Call to Arms: Course of Action

Militarily speaking, a Course of Action (COA) is a strategy that takes a plan from conception to action. Work with the Holy Spirit to create a COA for your household. This statement will anchor you to the authority you have in Christ, and help you wield it well in your home. (For reference purposes, I have included my own Course of Action on page 22. You may use it as an example, or ignore it altogether.)

1. Think about what you want your children to remember about their time in your home twenty years from now. What words or phrases do you hope come to their minds? How do you want them to feel when they look back on their time under your roof? Write those down.

2. Think about how your family currently spends the bulk of their free time. (Screens? Books? Board games? Nature hikes?) What is one tangible thing can you do as a family that will lead your children towards the words, phrases, and feelings you listed?

3. In what ways are you struggling with your God-given authority right now? Do the words of your mouth and meditations of your heart point your family to Jesus? If this is a point of struggle, write out biblically encouraging words to speak to your children, and refer back to them in times of frustration.

4. Look back at what you just wrote, and use the following statements as a template to write a Course of Action specific to your family's needs. *Our home will be a place of ___. I want my children to encounter ___ in our home. Our family will be passionate about ___. We will make ___ a priority by ___.* (Fill-in-the-blanks are just a jumping off point, don't feel limited to those specific statements.)

Robin's Course of Action

1. In 20 years, I want my children to remember a home filled with joy, love, laughter, and the power of prayer. Words and phrases I hope come to their minds include: "Mom and Dad fiercely loved us and pointed us to Jesus," and "We had such an adventure!" I want them to feel comfortable coming to us with every issue on their hearts and minds, to be secure in God's love, and passionate about leaving a legacy of faith.
2. We spend the bulk of our free time reading & exploring nature.
3. I'm currently struggling with the overwhelm of keeping our home in order, the demands of military duty, and homeschooling well. Biblical encouragement for my children: May you always grow in wisdom, stature, and favor with God and man. (Luke 2:52)
4. Our home will be a place where we encounter the risen, living Christ. Praise and prayer will permeate our walls. My sons will know the Word of God and routinely hear the Holy Spirit. We will prioritize joy, love, laughter, and the power of prayer. Our family will love fiercely and experience fun adventures. My husband and I will focus on building relationships so the boys will feel comfortable coming to us with every issue on their hearts and minds; will feel secure in God's love; and passionate about leaving a legacy of faith. In the midst of my responsibilities, I will make time for family read-alouds and nature hikes. Day in and day out, I will bless them with encouraging words. We will recite scripture, sing loud, and laugh long!

3. KNOW YOUR ENEMY

Stay alert! Watch out for your great enemy, the devil.
He prowls around like a roaring lion,
looking for someone to devour.
1 Peter 5:8 (NLT)

Your task will not be an easy one. Your enemy is well
trained, well equipped and battle-hardened.
He will fight savagely.
Dwight D. Eisenhower

My Air Force enlistment coincided with the early years of the Global War on Terror; I graduated Basic Training with National Defense and Global War on Terror medals, simply because I joined the military in a time of war. While I was shining my boots and practicing marching drills, some of my childhood friends were dodging bullets in Afghanistan and Iraq. The military spent copious amounts of time, energy, and resources to understand the adversary's tactics. Some of my earliest training memories involve anti-hijacking techniques, how *not* to get kidnapped by terrorists, and how to act in the unfortunate event that I do find myself in a hostage situation. Service members who put boots on the ground in the Middle East were well aware of methods used by terrorist fighters. Knowing your enemy is absolutely imperative.

Equally important in understanding who your enemy is, is understanding who your enemy is *not.* As a First Sergeant, I have dealt with many frustrated service members who were absolutely convinced their commander or supervisor was Public Enemy Number One. I've mediated countless counseling sessions where my goal was to help the service member see that the commanding officer wasn't maliciously trying to malign their careers or purposely thwart promotions. More often than not, strategic decisions made at top levels tend to be for the greater good, rather than a targeted "attack" on one particular person.

This also holds true in our families. There are times when it feels like our husband and kids are out to get us (undoubtedly there are times they feel the same about us as mothers), but the reality is they probably didn't sit down and plan a strategic assault on Mom. Satan—the Father of Lies—is your enemy, your family is not.

> *[The devil] was a murderer from the beginning, not holding to the truth, for there is no truth in him. When he lies, he speaks his native language, for he is a liar and the father of lies.* John 8:44b (NIV)

When my husband hurts my feelings, I have the choice to respond spitefully, or to extend grace. Rather than pointing out his shortcomings, I can ask him how his day went and genuinely listen to any frustration he needs to vent. My husband is not my enemy; I must see him as my ally.

When my oldest son blows up in anger, I have the option to yell back, or ask God to help me see his heart. Choosing a gentle answer over mom-wrath clears the path for life-giving conversation. After witnessing a meltdown of epic proportions by my youngest son, I must decide between a one-way ticket straight to his room (complete with a door slam), or asking him to share a snack with me on the patio. Rather than responding in a reactionary way, I can resolve to repair the relationship. My children are not my enemies; they have been entrusted to my care by the God of all Creation.

We meet King Jehoshaphat in the second book of Chronicles. He appointed good judges, fortified towns, and encouraged the people of Judah to follow God.

> *He appointed judges throughout the nation in all the fortified towns, and he said to them, "Always think carefully before pronouncing judgment. Remember that you do not judge to please people but to please the* LORD. *He will be with you when you render the verdict in each case. Fear the* LORD *and judge with integrity, for the* LORD *our God does not tolerate perverted justice, partiality, or the taking of bribes." In Jerusalem, Jehoshaphat appointed some of the Levites and priests and clan leaders in Israel to serve as judges for cases involving the* LORD'S *regulations and for civil disputes. These were his instructions to them: "You must always act in the fear of the* LORD, *with faithfulness and an undivided heart."* 2 Chronicles 19:5-9 (NLT)

In 2 Chronicles 20:1, surrounding nations declared war on Jehoshaphat. His response was to beg God for guidance, order a nation-wide fast, and engage in corporate prayer. Jehoshaphat chose to seek the Father's heart instead of immediately rushing out to attack the Moabites and Ammonites.

> *After this, the armies of the Moabites, Ammonites, and some of the Meunites declared war on Jehoshaphat...Jehoshaphat was terrified by this news and begged the* LORD *for guidance. He also ordered everyone in Judah to begin fasting...Jehoshaphat stood before the community of Judah and Jerusalem...He prayed, "O* LORD*, God of our ancestors, you alone are the God who is in heaven. You are ruler of all the kingdoms of the earth. You are powerful and mighty; no one can stand against you!"* 2 Chronicles 20:1-6 (NLT)

We are faced with a prowling adversary who waits to attack when we are weak. When Jesus woke Peter, James, and John from their prayer-naps in Matthew 26:41, He implored them to "keep watch and pray, so that [they would] not give in to temptation." Jesus knows your "spirit is willing, but [your] flesh is weak!" At the first sign of Satan's advance, we must choose to lean into Jesus instead of reacting in our own power.

Prayer

God, give me Your vision to clearly see when the enemy is working behind the scenes to derail my family's peace. In the heat of the moment, when my heart is wounded, fill my mouth with gentle words that turn away wrath. Help me to see my husband and children through Your eyes, and treat them accordingly. Thank You, Father, for loving me in spite of my failures and imperfections. In Jesus' awesome name, amen.

Call to Arms: Uniform Inspection

Historically, armies were distinguishable by the colors of their uniforms. The differences were obvious enough to let soldiers know where to aim. In the same way a soldier would understand his enemy's tactics and be able to identify their uniforms, it's important for you to understand who is undermining the peace in your home. This is where you get a good look at Satan's uniform, and an even better look at your family's true colors.

1. Read through the following verses: Genesis 3:1-5, Job 1:7, John 8:44, John 10:10, and 1 Peter 5:8. Write a list of Satan's characteristics.

____

____

____

____

____

____

____

____

____

____

____

____

____

____

____

____

____

2. Take a few minutes to look at a favorite photo of you and your husband together. Ask God to soften your heart towards him. Look at your husband through the lens of his Creator, and make a list of his positive characteristics.

3. Find cute photos of each of your children. As you look at these photos and recall special memories, ask God to show you your children through His eyes. Write a list of positive characteristics about each one of your children.

4. Review your family's list of positive characteristics, and contrast them with Satan's characteristics. Write out an anchoring statement you can hold onto when your family members act in ways that hurt your heart. Rather than responding from a place of wounding, take a moment to re-read this statement.

4. Develop a Strategy

Praise the LORD, *who is my Rock. He trains my hands for war and gives my fingers skill for battle.*
Psalm 144:1 (NLT)

There is no doubt that it is around the family and the home that all the greatest virtues, the most dominating virtues of human society, are created, strengthened, and maintained.
Winston Churchill

The weekend before Hurricane Katrina made landfall in 2005, I vividly remember standing amongst a group of medical officers, listening as rapid-fire plans and strategies took shape. At the time, we were preparing for every possible worst-case-scenario, but it was impossible to fathom the level of destruction that awaited the Gulf Coast. Shortly after Katrina made her way inland, the Army and Air Force had a line of military vehicles—

overflowing with supplies—waiting for clearance to cross the border from Texas to Louisiana.

Infrastructure damage made progress slow. Communication abilities were nearly non-existent. Lack of electricity left everyone in danger of heat-related casualties, on top of every other problem imaginable. We went straight to work, setting up an evacuation site at the convention center in New Orleans. My heart broke afresh with each bedraggled person we loaded onto the helicopters, yet I was amazed at the level of dedication and teamwork displayed by the thousands of military members who took part in the historic response.

No one sat back and lamented that the task was too difficult. No one complained of being bone-tired. After the evacuation portion of the mission, we set up an incredible tent hospital which provided life-saving capabilities in the storm-ravaged landscape. Our strategic training was put to the test, and proved its weight in gold. Tactics we had learned through the years did not fail us—they ensured we were prepared in the midst of chaos. Such strategies are imperative in motherhood; such strategies were practiced by Jesus.

Shortly after the Last Supper, Jesus took Simon Peter aside to prepare him for the coming storm.

> *Simon, Simon, Satan has asked to sift each of you like wheat. But I have pleaded in prayer for you, Simon, that your faith should not fail. So when you have repented and turned to me again, strengthen your brothers.*
> Luke 22:31-32 (NLT)

Jesus knew his faithful friend would falter, so he took three definitive actions to supernaturally prepare the way for Peter's restoration and redemption. First, He fervently prayed. Second, He spoke life-giving words. Third, He left Peter with a mission. We can take Christ's strategy straight into our homes, and put it in action with our own families. When faced with frustration, we can trade it for grace. Do as Jesus did: Plead for your family in prayer; speak life-giving words of affirmation to your husband and children on a daily basis; and give them a missional mindset rather than a legacy of feeling like they aren't enough.

In the midst of one of my deployments, my youngest son tearfully relayed that he missed me "welcoming him into the day." Confused by what he meant, I asked him to explain. "You know," he said, "when you come get me out of bed in the mornings, and smile at me to welcome me to the day." I had no idea how much that little act impacted my sweet son! Before your children's feet hit the floor each morning, be prepared to greet them with a smile and welcome them to the newly gifted day. Before their heads hit the pillow at night, fill their hearts with loving phrases they can hold on to in the days and years to come. Dream big over their lives, and tell them you're proud of them—not because of anything they have done or will do—simply because of who they are.

Prayer

God, thank You for loving me even though You know I will fail You. I'm in awe of Your overwhelming gift of grace. As I take Your words of truth to heart, fill me with encouraging words for each member of my family. Uproot every bitter seed from their hearts, and use me to plant life-giving words that will bear fruit through every future generation. In Jesus' beautiful name, amen.

Call to Arms: Strategic Preparation

What a blessing to see how Jesus strategically and lovingly prepared Simon Peter for what was to come. In the face of the cross, He was thinking about and praying for His disciples. Jesus modeled prayer, grace, forgiveness, and words of affirmation. Considering how Jesus prepared Peter, let's strategically prepare ourselves to face hardship at the hands of those we love.

1. Take a few minutes to imagine how you would like to be welcomed into each day. How your husband and children might like to be welcomed into their day. Write down some ideas to gracefully and lovingly welcome every member of your family into each newly gifted day.

2. How can you specifically pray for each member of your family? Ask God to show you where you need to "plead in prayer" as Jesus did for Peter. In what way(s) do you need the Holy Spirit to intercede to the Father on your behalf?

3. Write a biblical affirmation statement for each member of your household. Choose one person each morning to welcome into the day with a smile, hug, and their specific biblical affirmation. If you're able to do that with each family member all in one morning, go for it! If not, just focus on working your way through the family in a week's time.

4. Jesus charged Peter to strengthen his brothers after he faltered in his faith. What are some ways you can tangibly extend grace, forgiveness, and restoration to your family? How can you encourage them to focus on a missional mindset instead of dwelling on past hurts or frustrations?

5. Prepare for Battle

Use all the armor and weaponry that God provides, so that you will be able to stand against the deceptive tactics of the Adversary. For we are not struggling against human beings, but against rulers, authorities and cosmic powers governing this darkness, against the spiritual forces of evil in the heavenly realm. So take up every piece of war equipment God provides; so that when the evil day comes, you will be able to resist; and when the battle is won, you will be standing.
Ephesians 6:11-13 (CJB)

I remember my mother's prayers and they have always followed me. They have clung to me all my life.
Abraham Lincoln

My most intense days of training tend to involve lugging around a heavy rucksack that contains my chemical gear, Kevlar helmet, and vest. To be sure, the bag always gets lighter (to the point of emptiness) as I quickly put on every single piece of protective equipment. It all starts when someone yells, "GAS! GAS! GAS!" Years of training taught me the proper order to don and doff my gear. While it may appear chaotic, there's a definite method to the madness; each piece of equipment holds life-saving potential in the event of a chemical, biological, radiological, nuclear, or explosive event. In the same way military members have access to a full "battle rattle" that physically protects their bodies, we have access to spiritual protective gear that is far more powerful. Oftentimes, we're too busy or distracted to properly gear up, which leaves us vulnerable to an attack.

Ephesians 6 reminds us that God provides armor, weapons, and war equipment to ensure His victory is carried out on this earth. As a mother, *you* are a frontline warrior who has full access to these instruments of warfare. It is imperative that we take time every single day to put on the full armor of God. I would never show up for military duty without my uniform in order—without ensuring my insignia patches are correctly aligned and properly lacing up my combat boots. My uniform symbolizes the authority given to me by the United States Air Force. Your spiritual uniform, detailed in Ephesians, represents the authority you carry in Christ.

Therefore, stand! Have the belt of truth buckled around your waist, put on righteousness for a breastplate, and wear on your feet the readiness that comes from the Good News of shalom. Always carry the shield of trust, with which you will be able to extinguish all the flaming arrows of the Evil One. And take the helmet of deliverance; along with the sword given by the Spirit, that is, the Word of God; as you pray at all times, with all kinds of prayers and requests, in the Spirit, vigilantly and persistently, for all God's people.

Ephesians 6:14-18 (CJB)

With the belt of truth, refute the enemy's lies spoken over you, your husband, your children, and your home. The breastplate of righteousness is walking in obedience to God's commandments; it's making a daily choice to spend time with the Father in scripture and in prayer. Wearing the "shoes of shalom" goes far beyond our understanding of peace. It means walking out the Good News of the Prince of Peace in every situation we encounter. The deeply rooted meaning of *shalom* is revealed in Ancient Hebrew Pictographs. The *shin* character is a pictograph of teeth, which means to devour, consume, or destroy. The *lamed* character is a pictograph of a shepherd's staff, which represents authority and control. The *vav* character represents a tent peg or nail, and means to secure. Lastly, the *mem* character symbolizes water, waves, and chaos. To walk in God's shalom is *to destroy the authority that establishes chaos!* [1]

Other Bible translations refer to the shield of trust as "the shield of faith." Banking on Jesus' blood-bought victory is the ultimate shield of protection that will extinguish the enemy's flaming arrows. We fight from a place of victory, because Jesus has already defeated sin and death. With that knowledge, we put on the helmet of deliverance; our salvation has delivered us from the hands of the enemy. We must rely on the power of the Holy Spirit to protect our minds.

Up to this point, our spiritual battle gear has been defensive in nature. We don't take up the sword of the Spirit until *after* our protective gear is firmly in place. This is not a design flaw. The Word of God is our offensive measure, and cannot be properly used without already walking in truth, righteousness, shalom, trust, and deliverance. God's Word is the ultimate offensive weapon that decimates the enemy. We are to wield the sword of the Spirit as we pray at all times. It's not one or the other—they are to be

---

[1] https://hebrewwordpics.com/tag/shalom

used in tandem. Praying without ceasing, while advancing with the Word of God, supernaturally takes back territory the enemy has infiltrated.

> *We are human, but we don't wage war as humans do. We use God's mighty weapons, not worldly weapons, to knock down the strongholds of human reasoning and to destroy false arguments. We destroy every proud obstacle that keeps people from knowing God. We capture their rebellious thoughts and teach them to obey Christ.* 2 Corinthians 10:3-5 (NLT)

Prayer

God, give me an ever-increasing passion for Your Word. Through the power of Your Holy Spirit, teach me how to properly gear up each and every day. Show me how to shore up the defenses in my home so that my husband and children are also protected in the midst of battle. Forgive me for attempting to do things in my own power. Help me to rely on You for defense, deliverance, and dominion over the enemy. In Jesus' faithful name, amen.

used in tandem. Praying without ceasing, while advancing with the Word of God, supernaturally takes back territory the enemy has infiltrated.

> *We are human, but we don't wage war as humans do. We use God's mighty weapons, not worldly weapons, to knock down the strongholds of human reasoning and to destroy false arguments. We destroy every proud obstacle that keeps people from knowing God. We capture their rebellious thoughts and teach them to obey Christ.* 2 Corinthians 10:3-5 (NLT)

Prayer

God, give me an ever-increasing passion for Your Word. Through the power of Your Holy Spirit, teach me how to properly gear up each and every day. Show me how to shore up the defenses in my home so that my husband and children are also protected in the midst of battle. Forgive me for attempting to do things in my own power. Help me to rely on You for defense, deliverance, and dominion over the enemy. In Jesus' faithful name, amen.

Call to Arms: Bag Drag

Military members routinely perform "bag drags" where they empty the contents of their rucksacks to inspect each piece of equipment, ensuring everything is in proper working order. Metaphorically empty out your mind and heart at the feet of Jesus. Inspect your manner of speech, thought patterns, and habitual conduct. Are they in working order? Do they align with scripture?

1. When you reach the point of frustration, what words or phrases tend to be on your lips? Have you seen those mirrored back to you from your husband and children? Find a scripture in the previous pages to combat any words or phrases that are lies from the enemy. Write it below.

2. In times of exhaustion and overwhelm, where do your thoughts turn? What do you tell yourself? Is your internal dialogue healthy? If you've been echoing defeat from the adversary's mouth, find scriptures from the previous pages that refute negativity. Write them below.

3. When faced with stressful situations, how do you commonly respond? Write down your go-to responses—whether negative or positive. If stress leaves you feeling attacked by fiery arrows, sit with Jesus. Imagine Him holding up the shield of faith and trust in front of you when you feel too weak to lift it yourself.

4. Now that you've reflected on your normal responses to frustration, overwhelm, and stress, consider the areas you need God's freedom and grace. Write out a biblically healthy response, and spend time in prayer. Ask God to supernaturally meet your needs and bring His healing.

6. Secure the Perimeter

Like a city breached, without walls,
is a person who lacks self-control.
Proverbs 25:28 (CJB)

A pint of sweat saves a gallon of blood.
George S. Patton

One of the very first principles I learned in the military was the importance of securing the "entry control point." The ECP (because we'll use an acronym anytime we possibly can) is a militarized term for "door." We had dozens of drills that walked each recruit through a lengthy process of checking and double-checking identification before ever opening the door—even for someone we knew and easily recognized through the glass.

Heaven help the person who skipped any steps or opened the door prior to finishing the authentication process. It was a guaranteed way to earn midnight latrine duty, scrubbing already-gleaming tiles with an old toothbrush, only to be followed up by running laps until your legs turned to jelly. It's a mistake no one ever made twice, but the vast majority never made the mistake in the first place. The stakes were too high!

It's easy to understand why securing entry points earned such high importance early on in military training—it taught every single person to be vigilant. We all shared the burden of responsibility to keep one another safe. Refusing access to anyone with malicious intent is still a top priority on military installations worldwide. Teams of people are charged with checking fences, walls, gates, airways, and waterways to secure the perimeter at all times.

Nehemiah also understood this necessity. When he learned the walls and gates of Jerusalem had been destroyed, he mourned, fasted, and prayed (Nehemiah 1:3-4). As cupbearer to King Artaxerxes, Nehemiah's sadness was noticed right away; the king asked how he could help. Keep in mind that King Artaxerxes is Xerxes' son—the same Xerxes who made Esther queen. Nehemiah was serving Artaxerxes inside the fortress of Susa—the same place Esther was taken in Esther 2:8 (see page 5)!

Even though Artaxerxes was King Xerxes' son from one of his other wives, he was aware of his step-mother's plight to save her Jewish people. (Chronologically, Esther comes before Nehemiah; approximately 35 years separate the two biblical figures.[2]) In light of this, it's not difficult to see why King Artaxerxes allowed Nehemiah to return to Judah on a reconstruction mission. Decades earlier, Esther's obedience to God paved the way for Nehemiah! In the same way, your godly obedience prepares the way for future generations. When Nehemiah arrived in Jerusalem, he surveyed the damage, and later addressed the people.

[2] Rose Book of Bible Charts, Maps & Time Lines. Rose Publishing. 2015

But now I said to them, "You know very well what trouble we are in. Jerusalem lies in ruins, and its gates have been destroyed by fire. Let us rebuild the wall of Jerusalem and end this disgrace!"
Nehemiah 2:17 (NLT)

God's people, spurred on by Nehemiah's passion, began rebuilding the walls. Not everyone was happy with this progress. Soon, the Jewish people were harassed as they diligently worked on the ruins (Nehemiah 2:19). The enemy's opposition to Jerusalem's reconstruction reached fever pitch when they made plans to attack the Jewish people in the midst of the rebuild (Nehemiah 4:8). Nehemiah responded in prayer, and then did his part to secure the perimeter.

So I placed armed guards behind the lowest parts of the wall in the exposed areas. I stationed the people to stand guard by families, armed with swords, spears, and bows. Then as I looked over the situation, I called together the nobles and the rest of the people and said to them, "Don't be afraid of the enemy! Remember the L*ORD, who is great and glorious, and fight for your brothers, your sons, your daughters, your wives, and your homes!"*
Nehemiah 4:13-14 (NLT)

The people continued to face extreme opposition, but they didn't quit. Everyone went on guard duty, night and day. The perimeter remained secure at all times, with the responsibility being shared among families. They literally held a tool in one hand, and a weapon in the other.

Mama, this is your calling! You hug that baby with one hand, and grip your Bible in the other. Pray for your children as you wash their muddy laundry and clean their messy dishes. Ask God to bless the work of your husband's hands and feet as you pick up his socks off the floor. We see a powerful picture of this servant-warrior mindset as Nehemiah and his people carried their weapons with them at *all times*, even when they went on water breaks (Nehemiah 4:23).

Satan wants nothing more than for us to become weary in the midst of securing our family's perimeter: To give up a little territory here and there; to let screens be the babysitter; to disengage because the work never ceases; to live from a place of lack because no one seems to care. My battle cry is that you do not grow weary in doing good. Be an Esther for an upcoming Nehemiah. Your faithfulness today will bear a fruitful harvest in the not-so-distant future.

So let us not grow weary of doing what is good; for if we don't give up, we will in due time reap the harvest.
Galatians 6:9 (CJB)

This may seem like an impossible charge, but our resurrected Jesus makes the impossible *possible* every single day! The Holy Spirit longs to partner with you to rebuild the walls of your home. He has a vision, mission, and purpose for your family, and His plans far exceed anything we could imagine.

"For I know the plans I have for you," says the LORD. *"They are plans for good and not for disaster, to give you a future and a hope."* Jeremiah 29:11 (NLT)

Prayer

God, open my eyes to the spiritually porous places in our home. I repent for the holes I have created myself; for bringing destruction instead of renewal. In the name of Jesus and by His blood, I pray a divine hedge of protection over my family. Holy Spirit, heal our broken places and reestablish what the enemy has taken. Keep us spiritually vigilant as we partner with You to restore, rebuild, and repair. In Jesus' mighty name, amen.

Call to Arms: ID Check

Just as the military diligently checks credentials and identification, we should evaluate the "spiritual ID" of what we see, hear, and think before allowing entrance into the "doors" of our eyes, hearts, and minds. Whatever we allow into our lives as mothers affects our entire family.

1. Meditate on Philippians 4:4-8, then write down the identification credentials of what you should allow into your thoughts.

2. What have you allowed into your perimeter that does not pass the ID check? Whatever lies and negativity you permit will eventually end up directed at your family (and later redirected back at you). Make a list of negative thoughts you've struggled with in the past. Write the lies others have spoken about you, as well as those you've spoken over yourself.

3. Read Romans 8:9-17. These verses define your spiritual identity in Christ. Write a list of truths you can hold onto when the adversary's arrows are aimed at your heart, mind, home, and family. The enemy will bluff his way into your territory, and he'll stay there until you kick him out. Knowing who you are in Christ allows you to walk in His authority and fight from a place of victory.

4. Ask the Holy Spirit to reveal your strongholds that lead to unsecured perimeters. Using elements of your Motherhood Creed, write a prayer asking God to strengthen and secure your perimeters. This prayer will remind you of who you are in Christ, enabling you to take those thoughts captive.

Conclusion

Mamas, we don't need any more "self-help" or "self-love" books. We simply need the life-changing power of Jesus to infiltrate our lives, our families, and our homes, but we must invite Him over the threshold. If we're holding onto bitterness, anger, frustration—or clutching false identity papers—He won't just kick down the door and start flipping tables. We must first lay everything at His feet. He is waiting for us to release our grip on the enemy's inheritance of lies to receive His eternal inheritance of Truth.

Just as Jesus did with the paralytic man at the Pool of Bethesda (John 5:1-15), He's asking if you want to be healed. Are you ready to experience His freedom in motherhood? Ready to abandon whatever plagues you? This is the *only* point of surrender that will enable you to claim victory over the battle. Reach out. Grab His hand. Pick up your mat. Touch the hem of His cloak. Listen carefully, because this is His heart's cry over you:

> *Daughter, your faith has healed you. Go in peace and be freed from your suffering.* Mark 5:34 (NIV)

In accepting this mission of motherhood, you have raised your right hand and have been commissioned into service. You have all authority and power through Jesus—an authority which God entrusted to you that must never be abdicated. You know how to detect the enemy's tactics, and are empowered to develop scripture-based strategies to speak life over your family. You've partnered with the Holy Spirit, and are armed for battle on the home front. You are geared-up and equipped to secure your family's perimeter, thus protecting their inheritance. Jesus will take care of the resistance; you just have to arm up and show up, ready to wage war. He will fight for you!

We see an example of this in 2 Chronicles 20, when we meet Jahaziel. Back in Chapter 3, we met Jehoshaphat, who just so happens to be Jahaziel's king. In the midst of the king's prayer (see page 26), we see God move.

Then the Spirit of the LORD *came on Jahaziel…He said:*
"Listen, King Jehoshaphat and all who live in Judah and
Jerusalem! This is what the LORD *says to you: 'Do not be*
afraid or discouraged because of this vast army. For the
battle is not yours, but God's. Tomorrow march down
against them…You will not have to fight this battle.
Take up your positions; stand firm and see the deliverance
the LORD *will give you, Judah and Jerusalem. Do not be*
afraid; do not be discouraged. Go out to face them tomorrow,
and the LORD *will be with you.'"*
2 Chronicles 20:14-17 (NIV)

You are more than a conqueror, Brave Mama. Take up your position, stand firm, and watch as God supernaturally delivers your family. I'm praying you over the finish line!

Made in the USA
Middletown, DE
21 November 2022